Little Scholar
BIOLOGY

Christine Kimiko Dillard

Special thanks to Dr. Barbra Israel PhD

For Parents

Little Scholar: Biology is meant to grow with your child. The large titles and pictures will help expose infants to new words and help them form associations with those words. As your child grows and becomes a curious toddler, parents can incorporate the text explanations at the bottom of the page into the reading. The simple information can help the child grasp the basic concepts and definitions and start them on their journey into biology.

Biologists

are scientists who study living things.

They study
animals

Dogs, hamsters, and people are all animals.

Bugs are animals too!

Some animals have spines.
Spines are bony and are inside the body.
Animals with spines are called VERTEBRATES.

They study
plants

Flowers, trees, fruits and vegetables are all different kinds of plants.

Most plants have roots.
Roots grow in the soil and help the plant get food and water.
Plants with roots are called VASCULAR PLANTS.

They study
fungi

and other living things.

Bacteria

Mold

Another name for a living thing is an organism.
Organisms can be large and complex or small and simple.
Some are so small you cannot see them, like **BACTERIA**.

They study
you

You are alive.
Yay!

You are part of a group called homo sapiens.
Homo sapiens have two legs, two arms, and walk upright.
Grouping based on similarities is called **CLASSIFICATION**.

Biologists

study what living things need.

Living things need
water

Living things need water because they are made of water.

In fact, over half of your body is just water!

Water can take three different forms.
These forms are gas, liquid, and solid.
The water you drink is in the form of a **LIQUID**.

Living things need
energy

Animals get energy by eating food.

Energy allows us to do things.

Plants make their own food.
They use water, carbon dioxide and sunlight.
This process is called **PHOTOSYNTHESIS**.

Living things need

oxygen

Oxygen can be found in water, dirt and air.

Many animals breathe in oxygen from the air.
The air surrounds the planet and has different layers.
The layers of air are called the **ATMOSPHERE**.

Biologists

study how living things are built.

Living things are built from

cells

Cells are the building blocks of all living things!

Animal cells have an outer layer called a cell membrane.
The cell membrane holds the cell together.
The inside of a cell is made of parts called ORGANELLES.

Living things are built from

tissue

When the same kind of cells work together they make tissue!

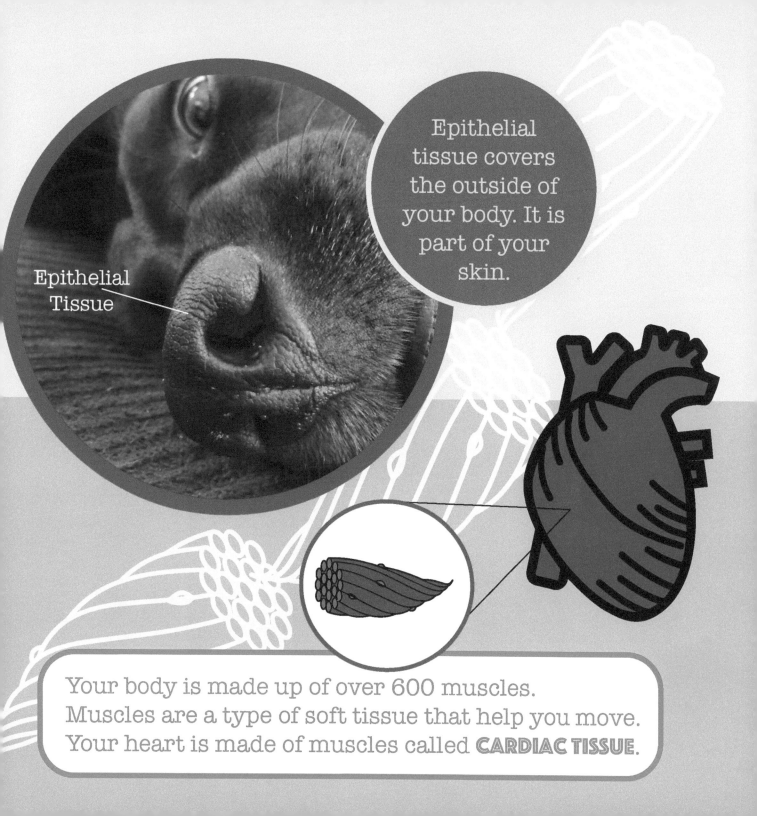

Epithelial
Tissue

Epithelial tissue covers the outside of your body. It is part of your skin.

Your body is made up of over 600 muscles. Muscles are a type of soft tissue that help you move. Your heart is made of muscles called **CARDIAC TISSUE**.

Living things are built from

organs

Groups of tissues make organs. Your stomach is an organ.

A very important organ in your body is the brain. The brain allows you to think and control your body. It sends orders to your body with cells called **NEURONS**.

Biologists

study how living things are part of the world.

A living thing is part of
biodiversity

Plant

Caterpiller

Aphid

Bear

All the living things together make up the biodiversity of this pond.

How many diffrent living things do you see?

All living things need other living things to survive. You need plants to make the air you breathe. Living things interact together forming **ECOSYSTEMS**.

A living thing is part of a
food chain

A bug eats a plant. A lizard eats the bug. A bird eats the lizard. You eat the bird. Welcome to the food chain!

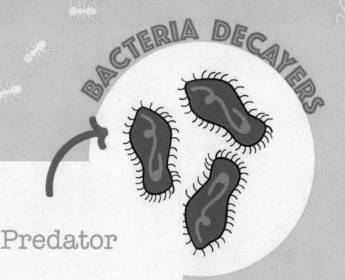

BACTERIA DECAYERS

Predator

Eaters

The food chain shows how energy and nutrients move from one living thing to another.

Makers

Food chains are divided into trophic levels. These are groups of makers, eaters and decayers. Eaters who eat other eaters, like you, are **PREDATORS**.

A living thing is part of a
biome

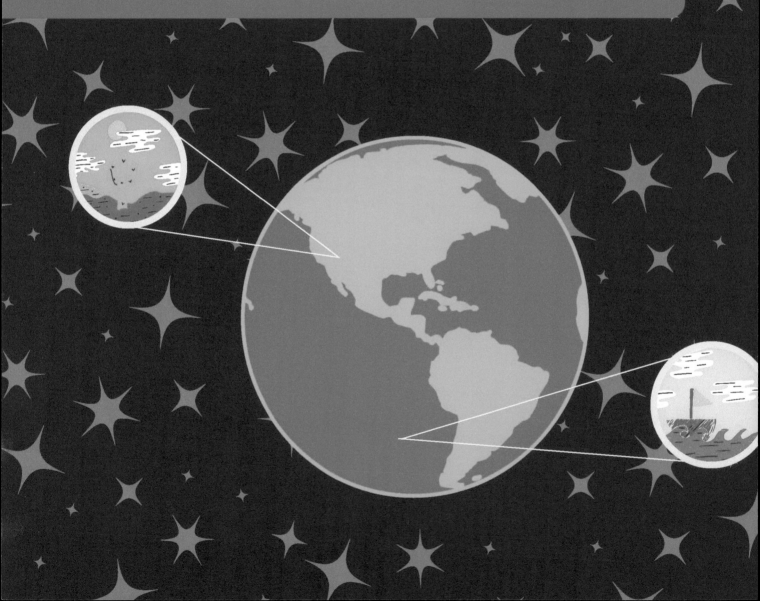

Biomes are places that are alike and are home to living things.

Jungles, deserts, oceans, and grasslands are all biomes!

People are home to tiny living things called microbes. Bacteria and other microbes live all over your body. This makes YOU a biome called a **MICROBIOME**.

A living thing is part of the
biosphere

The biosphere is where living things exist on our planet.

You live in the biosphere!

Creatures on the ocean floor live in the seabed hydrosphere. The lowest point is over 6 miles below the ocean's surface. This cold, dark place is called the MARIANA TRENCH.

Biologists

study

BIOLOGY

the study of living things.

If you enjoyed this book,
please share a review on amazon.com

Find more books by Christine Kimiko Dillard at
www.storytimehouse.com

My First Math Book
My First Math Book: Counting

Coming soon...
Goizaimon and the Railroad
Little Green and Little Red
Little Scholar: Biology Stories

CPSIA information can be obtained
at www.ICGtesting.com
Printed in the USA
LVHW072302280419
615902LV00017B/267/P